T0194405

Poetry-N-Motion

The Devotional

Marcel.

authorHOUSE®

AuthorHouse™
1663 Liberty Drive
Bloomington, IN 47403
www.authorhouse.com
Phone: 1-800-839-8640

First published by AuthorHouse   01/21/2012

ISBN: 978-1-4685-2807-7 (sc)
ISBN: 978-1-4685-2806-0 (hc)
ISBN: 978-1-4685-2808-4 (ebk)

Library of Congress Control Number: 2011962667

Printed in the United States of America

Contents

Photo by: Perry Alliman

In picture from left to right: Paul Falcone, Nate Wagner, Travis Fielder, Logan Barnhill, Waytt Saint, Brian Riekenderg, Brian Earley, and Lee Berry

Acknowledgments

I would like to thank God the Father for all things. He gave me great fellowship with so many people and "The Gift" to bring His vision to reality. I would like to also thank my siblings (Howard, Liz and Cil) as they helped shape me into the man I am today. There are so many brethren who through their fellowship enrich my life, just to name a few (Wyat Saint, Logan Barnhill, Lewis Hudson, Allen Simmons, Perry Alliman, Kurt, Art, Travis Fielder, Phil Montag, Chris Hazell, both Brians, and so many more). I'd

Marcel.

like to add a very special thanks to my parents (Howard and Sandra Harrison) who, when I wanted to give up, pushed me on.

Dedication

This book is dedicated to God the Father, as He is the reason for my existence, along with Sandra E. Harrison my dearly departed mother and to all my friends and family that have supported me and believed in me all these years.

Preface

Welcome to my world. I plan to take you on a journey through my mind. Over the years I have been blessed with the gift of words. Such a great form of expression the Lord has entrusted me with. As I try to be a good steward of the gifts the Father has given me I am sharing my thoughts with all of you. When you read the song or poem I would like you to get a vivid mental picture of the events and concepts that I deal with in these writings. It is my hope that these creations will have a wide range of appeal that you can relate to. Keeping this in mind we will look at the ultimate

Marcel.

creative writing experience done by the master creator (God the Father). I invite you to make yourself comfortable grab your Bible and enjoy the ride . . . .

My World

Welcome to my world
Are you ready to take a trip
Are you ready for the ride
I don't know where I am going
Get ready . . .
Step inside
Look into my soul
Take a look what do you find
A fire burns
a passion roars

Marcel.

How can I quench this thirst
Where is my relief
There is a guiding light
There is a force in power
He is always with me
You ask me who this is
The one with the son Who sacrificed all
For a wanton race
Who in His face Will flaunt it all

Who Will You Pray For Tonight

who will you pray for tonight
so many so strong
so many how long
will we have this struggle
when will we see the light
of day
the break of dawn
who will leave next
how often to sing
this morning song

I'll pray for you
will you pray for me
from one friend to the next

Marcel.

so many are called
next to me
now time stands still
looking into this field
of vision
of forbearing hindsight
twenty twenty
nourish the memories
of friends now silent

bring it to the forefront
bring it to the light
the pain you feel
looming in the night
remember the faces
the laughter
the smile
keep the light burning
keep the essence alive
for the higher ground we strive
to subdue the specter
to subside the pain

the morning after
the sun will rise
we sit in silence
this is right
that is wrong
our beliefs still run strong
now reality sets in
this is the course of life
a fallen tear reflects the light
now time to grieve
remembrance is hindsight

Marcel.

As illustrated in these verses, prayer is paramount to building a strong relationship with the Lord. Prayer is an awesome tool and our direct connection to our father.

Confess [your] faults one to another, and pray one for another, that ye may be healed. The effectual fervent prayer of a righteous man availeth much.

James 5:16b

⁸The sacrifice of the wicked [is] an abomination to the LORD: but the prayer of the upright [is] his delight.

Proverbs 15:8

¹And he spake a parable unto them [to this end], that men ought always to pray, and not

to faint; ²Saying, There was in a city a judge, which feared not God, neither regarded man: ³And there was a widow in that city; and she came unto him, saying, Avenge me of mine adversary. ⁴And he would not for a while: but afterward he said within himself, though I fear not God, nor regard man; ⁵yet because this widow troubleth me, I will avenge her, lest by her continual coming she weary me. ⁶And the Lord said, Hear what the unjust judge saith. ⁷And shall not God avenge his own elect, which cry day and night unto him, though he bear long with them?

Luke 18:1-7

We have all dealt with pain. Prayer along with Christian fellowship helps us cope ushering in His comforter to our aid.

[31]Then had the churches rest throughout all Judaea and Galilee and Samaria, and were edified; and walking in the fear of the Lord, and in the comfort of the Holy Ghost, were multiplied.

Acts 9:31

[15]If ye love me, keep my commandments. [16]And I will pray the Father, and he shall give you another Comforter that he may abide with you forever; [17][Even] the Spirit of truth; whom the world cannot receive, because it seeth

him not, neither knoweth him: but ye know him; for he dwelleth with you, and shall be in you.

John 14:15-17

Dig Deep

Dip deep
what do you feel
dig deep
now don't break the seal
dig deep
just listen to me
you've got to dig deep
take breath
dig deep
take breath
do you feel a little weak
now stop . . . .
pay attention to me
you've got to dig deep
dig deep

a little deeper now
dig deep
a little weaker now
dig deep
let Him in now
dig deep . . . .
break it down
dig deep
lay it down
dig deep
take the crown
dig deep you choose
dig deep
what will you lose
dig deep
you'll see
dig deep
follow me

★ ★ ★

At some point in our lives we all have to look deep to see what we have inside. We have to make that choice of who our allegiance is to. As Christians, we know a crown of glory awaits us!!! These verses will help keep that thought fresh in our minds.

²⁴Then said Jesus unto his disciples, If any [man] will come after me, let him deny himself, and take up his cross, and follow me.

Mathew 16:24

⁴And when the chief Shepherd shall appear, ye shall receive a crown of glory that fadeth not away.

1 Peter 5:4

[12]Blessed [is] the man that endureth temptation: for when he is tried, he shall receive the crown of life, which the Lord hath promised to them that love him.

James 1:12

NOTES

Mirror Mirror

The pain inside it takes hold
the pleasure builds
the map unfolds
line them up
all your fears in a row
brace yourself
gonna be a bumpy ride
into the looking glass
the blemishes you cannot hide
mirror mirror on the wall
look at me now
o how did I fall
did you see me
did you hear His call
why didn't you warn me

let me know my fate
mirror mirror
why did you hesitate
there was a time shattered by my youth
didn't really take a stand
didn't listen to the truth
looking back I see
the danger all around
kept my chin up
I held my own
then the taste
my world was blown
mirror mirror now I see
the lessons I've learned

the tides of that which must be
you didn't warn the fool
we all must live and learn
the touch of His love has saved yet
another
now the hearts and minds must be
turned

Marcel.

As we look in the mirror what do we see, the good, bad and ugly? It is important to realize our flaws, admit them, put them before the Father and learn to forgive ourselves. We need to let the guilt go so we can experience the feeling of forgiveness and grace from the Father. This will allow us to be ready and hear His call.

²Wash me thoroughly from mine iniquity, and cleanse me from my sin. ³For I acknowledge my transgressions: and my sin [is] ever before me.

Psalms 51:2-3

⁹If we confess our sins, he is faithful and just to forgive us [our] sins, and to cleanse us from all unrighteousness.

1 John 1:9

¹⁴How much more shall the blood of Christ, who through the eternal Spirit offered himself without spot

Hope

When I look outside my window
I see a world ready to be taken
Often unsure how or when
I Know the answer lies within
When your world seems to be
crashing down
Hold true to your faith
Look inside yourself and you will find
The strength to go on
The power to keep your head up
The will to be strong
Through the adversity

Marcel.

Through all of the rain
You will make it through
You can make it through the pain
Just keep the hope alive
Never give up on the dream
For what does not kill us
Will make us stronger
This is the way of life
It seems

Hope is one of the most important things a Christian can possess. We have faith in our Father and His son. We also have great hope for the things to come. Let's look at these verses and **keep our Christian hope alive!**

⁸I have set the LORD always before me: because [he is] at my right hand, I shall not be moved. ⁹Therefore my heart is glad, and my glory rejoiceth: my flesh also shall rest in hope.

Psalms 16:8-9

⁸But let us, who are of the day, be sober, putting on the breastplate of faith and love; and for an helmet, the hope of salvation.

I Thessalonians 5:8

¹⁶Now our Lord Jesus Christ himself, and God, even our Father, which hath loved us, and hath given [us] everlasting consolation and good

hope through grace, [17]Comfort your hearts, and stablish you in every good word and work.

II Thessalonians 2:16

NOTES

Night (She)

The night she falls
She covers the land
She blankets the sea in her shadowy
band she sees the follies of
drunken man
She takes the chance for dawn is close
at hand
She houses the stars glimmering in
her might
She makes no apologies She fears
not the light

Marcel.

She is bold and brazen A fearsome foe
Giving wrath to the moon's
piercing glow
But do not fear her in all of her might
For the day is but the absence of night

We know we are children of the day or light. Let's take a look at these verses and meditate a moment.

⁵Ye are all the children of light, and the children of the day: we are not of the night, nor of darkness. ⁶Therefore let us not sleep, as [do] others; but let us watch and be sober. ⁷For they that sleep, sleep in the night; and they that be drunken are drunken in the night. ⁸But let us, who are of the day, be sober, putting on the breastplate of faith and love; and for an helmet, the hope of salvation.

1 Thessalonians 5:5-8

⁵And there shall be no night there; and they need no candle, neither light of the sun; for the Lord God giveth them light: and they shall reign forever and ever.

Revelation 22:5

Walk In My Shoes

Wanna walk in my shoes
Wanna be like me
Wanna walk in my shoes
Wanna see what I see
Take a walk in my shoes
See the world through my eyes
Take a walk in my shoes You'd be
surprised what's that name
Who's that face
Can't remember who won the race
Hold it in
just don't talk
Keep that secret
Try to walk the walk
What did I feel

Marcel.

Who did I tell
Were you with me
When I last fell
Can't break these chains
Don't know why
Keep those shoes
A kiss goodbye
Don't change your shoes
Try to keep them clean
Don't track dirt On the grass so green
Just don't ask To see what I've seen
Walk in your shoes the way you will
Put it on my tab
You'll pay the bill
Take those shoes Keep them clean
Did I see dirt on the grass that's green
Open your eyes you just might see
The other side is not so green

Sometimes it seems everyone else is better off than we are. We see so many people seemingly excelling to great heights in the world as we just stand still. It is so very important for us to be content with what we have giving thanks to God for all.

⁵Perverse disputings of men of corrupt minds, and destitute of the truth, supposing that gain is godliness: from such withdraw thyself. ⁶But godliness with contentment is great gain. ⁷For we brought nothing into [this] world, [and it is] certain we can carry nothing out.

1 Timothy 6:5-7

¹⁵And he said unto them, Take heed, and beware of covetousness: for a man's life consisteth not in the abundance of the things which he possesseth.

Luke 12:15

[18]In everything give thanks: for this is the will of God in Christ Jesus concerning you.

1 Thessalonians 5:18

NOTES

Strife

---

faceless

nameless

spreading through the sea

crouching . . .

waiting . . .

looking to be set free

listening with open ears

waiting for the moment to be

seize it

take it by the horns

a whisper in the ear

a glance out of text

pass it on

tell it to the next

rolling and building

distorting the truth
do you listen to the lies uttered in youth
my name is strife
I lie in wait
you foolish mortals
so many chances for me to take
as long as you are in the flesh
as long as you are weak
I will be there to creep
into your hearts
your little minds
into your lives
is where I will find
room to grow
room to move
until you find the strength to let me go

Strife is something we **must** fight. This can enter our homes, churches, jobs and relationships. These verses should help us to be aware of and combat this potential stumbling block in our lives.

28A froward man soweth strife: and a whisperer separateth chief friends.

Proverbs 16:28

1Better [is] a dry morsel and quietness therewith, than an house full of sacrifices [with] strife.

14The beginning of strife [is as] when one letteth out water: therefore leave off contention, before it be meddled with.

19He loveth transgression that loveth strife: [and] he that exalteth his gate seeketh destruction.

Proverbs 17:1, 14, 19

Together

Bring it together
we gotta get it together
we gotta get it together
what are we here for
what will we do
where will we go
let's get it together
let's try to get it straight

life on the streets
look at this side
what does it mean
when we don't have enough to eat
cold and hungry
they sit alone

Marcel.

who will care for them
man . . . I don't know

life in the sky
penthouse living must be nice
don't look down on the street
don't say hi, you just might meet
one of these
homeless and alone
not your problem
I have my cell phone

in the middle of the night
do you hear their cries
the pacing footsteps
where do you live
are you high in the sky
or night is it you who cry

life on the streets
do you know how it feels
take a look around you
LOOK AT IT
life . . .
yeah, it's real

Marcel.

Man, this one really tugs at my core. The plight of the poor is a resounding theme throughout mankind's history. One of the strongest desires inside of me is to help those in need. We should be thankful always for what the Lord has given us, being cheerful givers to those less fortunate than ourselves. It is very unproblematic to go through life focusing on our wants and needs. These verses should help bring to the front of our minds what the lord wants us to do concerning the poor.

34Then shall the King say unto them on his right hand, Come, ye blessed of my Father, inherit the kingdom prepared for you from the foundation of the world: 35For I was an hungred, and ye gave me meat: I was thirsty, and ye gave me drink: I was a stranger, and ye took me in: 36Naked, and ye clothed me: I was sick, and ye visited me: I was in prison, and ye came unto me. 37Then shall the righteous answer him, saying, Lord, when saw we thee an hungred, and fed [thee]? or thirsty, and gave [thee] drink? 38When saw we thee a stranger, and took [thee] in? or naked, and clothed [thee]? 39Or when saw we thee sick, or in prison, and came unto thee? 40And the King shall answer and say unto them, Verily

I say unto you, Inasmuch as ye have done [it] unto one of the least of these my brethren, ye have done [it] unto me.

Mathew 25:34-40

[6]But this [I say], He which soweth sparingly shall reap also sparingly; and he which soweth bountifully shall reap also bountifully. [7]Every man according as he purposeth in his heart, [so let him give]; not grudgingly, or of necessity: for God loveth a cheerful giver.

II Corinthians 9:6-7

Broken

Broken on the floor
just take a little step
not again to soar
just forget the past but always learn
have to keep moving on
I have to be strong

there is the face I used to long for
wanted with my soul
just to have a little more
time and devotion
love and emotion
time to let it go
time to let life flow

Marcel.

broken heart
clouded mind
fighting temptation trying to unwind
picking up the pieces of this shattered
dream
this foolish vision as right as it seemed
leap over the block get back on track
now pressing on
no, can't look back

just beginning to rise
getting my strength back
no longer listening to the cries
of a wounded heart
or scattered mind
pressing to the goal
the power somehow I know I will find

We have all been broken in some way or another. Whether that love we lost, that shattered dream or that big promotion the other guy got. If we remember to seek His kingdom first, He will take care of the rest.

²³The life is more than meat, and the body [is more] than raiment. ²⁴Consider the ravens: for they neither sow nor reap; which neither have storehouse nor barn; and God feedeth them: how much more are ye better than the fowls? ²⁵And which of you with taking thought can add to his stature one cubit? ²⁶If ye then be not able to do that thing which is least, why take ye thought for the rest? ²⁷Consider the lilies how they grow: they toil not, they spin not; and yet I say unto you, that Solomon in all his glory was not arrayed like one of these. ²⁸If then God so clothe the grass, which is to day in the field, and tomorrow is cast into the oven; how much more [will he clothe] you, O ye of little faith? ²⁹And seek not ye

what ye shall eat, or what ye shall drink, neither be ye of doubtful mind. [30]For all these things do the nations of the world seek after: and your Father knoweth that ye have need of these things? [31]But rather seek ye the kingdom of God; and all these things shall be added unto you.

Luke 12: 23-31

If you would, consider with me Job. For this I would like you to **read the entire book of Job**. The only other figure in the bible I can think of more broken than Job was Jesus Christ himself. Enough said.

NOTES

It's Not Easy

No it's not easy for me
it is not easy to be
the man I want to be
why does he elude me
why can't I see
when will you release me
please, don't you understand
this is not of my hands

this is not what I want to be
forgive the trespass
I think you know the heart of me
my tongue is harsh

Marcel.

my actions tattered
laugh it off
leave the mess scattered

the breach that lies at the heart
the kindness beneath I can barely see
the good that somehow I manage to do
just seems to wither in the sight of you
no! It is not easy this way
after I have spoken what do I say

The Father never promised this life following His son would be easy. The sin nature in the flesh is at constant war with the spiritual man/woman within us. Taking a look at these verses should help us to realize we are not alone. We are not the first nor will be the last to go through trials in this struggle in the service of our lord. However, the Lord will help us.

¹Now about that time Herod the king stretched forth [his] hands to vex certain of the church. ²And he killed James the brother of John with the sword. ³And because he saw it pleased the Jews, he proceeded further to take Peter also. (Then were the days of unleavened bread.) ⁴And when he had apprehended him, he put [him] in prison, and delivered [him] to four quaternions of soldiers to keep him; intending after Easter to bring him forth to the people. ⁵Peter therefore was kept in prison: but prayer was made without ceasing of the church unto God for him. ⁶And when Herod would have brought him forth, the same night Peter was sleeping between two soldiers, bound with two chains: and the

keepers before the door kept the prison. [7]And, behold, the angel of the Lord came upon [him], and a light shined in the prison: and he smote Peter on the side, and raised him up, saying, Arise up quickly. And his chains fell off from [his] hands.

Acts 12:1-7

[1]Now there were in the church that was at Antioch certain prophets and teachers; as Barnabas, and Simeon that was called Niger, and Lucius of Cyrene, and Manaen, which had been brought up with Herod the tetrarch, and Saul. [2]As they ministered to the Lord, and fasted, the Holy Ghost said, Separate me Barnabas and Saul

for the work whereunto I have called them. ³And when they had fasted and prayed, and laid [their] hands on them, they sent [them] away. ⁴So they, being sent forth by the Holy Ghost, departed unto Seleucia; and from thence they sailed to Cyprus. ⁵And when they were at Salamis, they preached the word of God in the synagogues of the Jews: and they had also John to [their] minister. ⁶And when they had gone through the isle unto Paphos, they found a certain sorcerer, a false prophet, a Jew, whose name [was] Barjesus: ⁷Which was with the deputy of the country, Sergius Paulus, a prudent man; who called for Barnabas and Saul, and desired to hear the word of God. ⁸But Elymas the sorcerer (for so is his name by interpretation) withstood them, seeking to turn away the deputy from the faith. ⁹Then Saul, (who also [is called] Paul,) filled with the Holy Ghost, set his eyes on him, ¹⁰And said, O full of all subtlety and all mischief, [thou] child of the devil, [thou] enemy of all righteousness, wilt thou not cease to pervert the right ways of the Lord? ¹¹And now, behold, the hand of the Lord [is] upon thee, and thou shalt be blind, not seeing the sun for a season. And immediately there fell on him a mist and a darkness; and he went about seeking some to lead him by the hand.

Acts 13:1-11

NOTES

The Price Of Fame

Another city
another place to be
another day on the road
so many deadlines to meet
another show
so many more faces
but who knows the real me
this is what I love
I have finally made the cut
running through my veins
doing what I love

Marcel.

the hours in the day just don't
seem to last
all the work ahead
all the decisions
man it all moves so fast
but when you step on that stage
you hear the roar of crowd
you see the smiling faces
then after you take your bow
you remember why you started
and nothing can stop you now

Whether you are a construction worker or an entertainer God expects us to use our talents and abilities to the fullest for Him. It is so easy to put Him on the back burner in this hectic rat race. These verses will help us to remember to make time for the lord remembering always all we have He gave us, and not to let idols enter our hearts such as money, cars, career or even family.

⁷For every one of the house of Israel, or of the stranger that sojourneth in Israel, which separateth himself from me, and setteth up his idols in his heart, and putteth the stumbling block of his iniquity before his face, and cometh to a prophet to enquire of him concerning me; I the LORD will answer him by myself: ⁸And I will set my face against that man, and will make him a sign and a proverb, and I will cut him off from the midst of my people; and ye shall know that I [am] the LORD.

Ezekiel 14:7-8

¹⁴For [the kingdom of heaven is] as a man travelling into a far

country, [who] called his own servants, and delivered unto them his goods. [15]And unto one he gave five talents, to another two, and to another one; to every man according to his several ability; and straightway took his journey. [16]Then he that had received the five talents went and traded with the same, and made [them] other five talents. [17]And likewise he that [had received] two, he also gained other two. [18]But he that had received one went and digged in the earth, and hid his lord's money. [19]After a long time the lord of those servants cometh, and reckoneth with them. [20]And so he that had received five talents came and brought other five talents, saying, Lord, thou deliveredst unto me five talents:

behold, I have gained beside them five talents more. ²¹His lord said unto him, Well done, [thou] good and faithful servant: thou hast been faithful over a few things, I will make thee ruler over many things: enter thou into the joy of thy lord. ²²He also that had received two talents came and said, Lord, thou deliveredst unto me two talents: behold, I have gained two other talents beside them. ²³His lord said unto him, Well done, good and faithful servant; thou hast been faithful over a few things, I will make thee ruler over many things: enter thou into the joy of thy lord. ²⁴Then he which had received the one talent came and said, Lord, I knew thee that thou art an hard man, reaping where thou hast not sown, and gathering where thou hast not strawed: 25And I was afraid, and went and hid thy talent in the earth: lo, [there] thou hast [that is] thine. 26His lord answered and said unto him, [Thou] wicked and slothful servant, thou knewest that I reap where I sowed not, and gather where I have not strawed: 27Thou oughtest therefore to have put my money to the exchangers, and [then] at my coming I should have received mine own with usury. 28Take therefore the talent from him, and give [it] unto him which hath ten talents. 29For unto every one that hath shall be given, and he shall have abundance: but from him that hath not shall be taken away even that which he hath. 30And cast ye the unprofitable servant into outer darkness: there shall be weeping and gnashing of teeth.

Mathew 25:14-30

[29]For the gifts and calling of God [are] without repentance.

Romans 11:29

We know that an idol [is] nothing in the world, and that [there is] none other God but one.

I Corinthians 8:4b

³Thou shalt have no other gods before me.

Exodus 20:3

The Blackness

The blackness starts
Creeping in; it catches you unaware
Little by Little it takes hold
of your heart . . . .
of your mind . . . .
It masquerades as a friend
to bring a little joy
It plays with your soul
As if you were his little toy
He'll show his face in the ones you love
All part of the game

Marcel.

The only defense we have is the Son
of light
Arm yourself with words of truth
Let not the evil one steal your heart
Break his hold
In the place the blackness starts

I believe we live in a very spiritually alive time. We have to stay alert for our enemies can be very subtle. As Christians we need to be aware of the influences we allow into our lives. What we let in can influence what comes out of us.

[3]For though we walk in the flesh, we do not war after the flesh: [4](For the weapons of our warfare [are] not carnal, but mighty through God to the pulling down of strong holds)

2 Corinthians 10:3-4

[8]Be sober, be vigilant; because your adversary the devil, as

a roaring lion, walketh about, seeking whom he may devour:

1 Peter 5:8

¹⁰And he called the multitude, and said unto them, Hear, and understand: ¹¹Not that which goeth into the mouth defileth a man; but that which cometh out of the mouth, this defileth a man.

¹⁵Then answered Peter and said unto him, Declare unto us this parable. ¹⁶And Jesus said, Are ye also yet without understanding? ¹⁷Do not ye yet understand that whatsoever entereth in at the mouth goeth into the belly, and is cast out into the draught? ¹⁸But those things which proceed out of

the mouth come forth from the heart; and they defile the man. [19]For out of the heart proceed evil thoughts, murders, adulteries, fornications, thefts, false witness, blasphemies: [20]these are [the things] which defile a man: but to eat with unwashen hands defileth not a man.

Mathew 15:10-11, 15-20

NOTES

Sometimes

Sometimes I feel so alone
as if I am wondering without a home
I feel like I am out of place
I do not want to be here
I don't want to run this race
sometimes I lose a little faith
I forget the promise
it lies deep within me
the desire for these things
surely this must mean
that they will all come to pass
the hopes
the dreams
my life's work
the visions of accomplishment

then sometimes a friend will share
a thought
the wonderful insight
it wakes me up
never will I forget who brought me here
who gave me these things
I know what my life does
and is going to mean
my friend of long ago
did you know when you share
your understanding
you make my heart grow
the war is raging deep inside my soul
for life
for love
for knowledge
for integrity

please help me to let it show
thank you for this friend
out of nowhere this knowledge appears
a familiar face
someone to talk to
thank you for knowing
and reminding me what I have to do

Marcel.

We know this world system is not our home. We have temporary lodging here. We are just passing through. Sometimes we feel alone, but we have to remember God is always with us. He knows what it is like to be in the flesh. He gave us each other to help us along the way along with His comforter. Looking at these verses should comfort and remind us.

19"If you were of the world, the world would love its own. Yet because you are not of the world, but I chose you out of the world, therefore the world hates you."

John 15:19

20"But our citizenship is in heaven. And we eagerly await a Savior from there, the Lord Jesus Christ"

Philippians 3:20

15If ye love me, keep my commandments. 16And I will pray the Father, and he shall give you another Comforter, that he may abide with you for ever; 17[Even] the Spirit of truth; whom the world cannot receive, because it seeth him not, neither knoweth him: but ye know him; for he dwelleth with you, and shall be in you.

John 14:15-17

[17]For, behold, I create new heavens and a new earth: and the former shall not be remembered, nor come into mind.

Isaiah 65:17

The Gift

The gift is there for you and me
The future
Open your eyes so you can see
Don't you realize what you can be
In your heart lies His tree
It's waiting there for you
Make the choice
You know what you have to do
The gift

Marcel.

We know the greatest gift given to mankind is the tree of life in the person of **JESUS CHRIST.** How many of you would give your only son's life for "a wanton race who in your face would flaunt it all"? There is one verse that says it all!!!!

For God so loved the world, that he gave his only begotten Son, that whosoever believeth in him should not perish, but have everlasting life.

John 3:16

NOTES

This book is my gift to the reader. We have taken a journey through my thoughts and feelings that the Lord has so graciously allowed me to put to words. I am so grateful to our Father for giving me this avenue of expression.

It is my true desire that this devotional book has helped, in some way, all who read it. If you enjoyed these lyrics and poems keep an eye and ear open for the forthcoming album "The Gift". God willing I will set these writings to music for your listening pleasure.

Thank you for your time and love for our heavenly Father and His word!

Until next time,
MARCEL.

Marcel.

P. S.

Thank you Father for my fellow servant **Gale E. Solomon.** The great tool you used to spur me on to finally bring this vision you gave me to come forth.

Who will you pray for tonight?

"Pray without ceasing" I Thessalonians 5:17

Photo by Perry Alliman
Pictured from left to right front row: Paul
Falcone, Lewis Hudson, Brian Riekenberg,
and Brian Earley Back row: Logan Barnhill,
Nate Wagner, Wyatt Saint, Travis Fielder,
and Lee Berry